MW00886514

IF FOUND PLEASE RETURN TO:

_____
_____
_____
EMAIL: _____
REWARD: _____

JULY 2022 - JUNE 2023

2022 - 2023

July

S	M	T	W	T	F	S
					1	2
3	4	5	6	7	8	9
10	11	12	13	14	15	16
17	18	19	20	21	22	23
24	25	26	27	28	29	30
31						

August

S	M	T	W	T	F	S
	1	2	3	4	5	6
7	8	9	10	11	12	13
14	15	16	17	18	19	20
21	22	23	24	25	26	27
28	29	30	31			

September

S	M	T	W	T	F	S
				1	2	3
4	5	6	7	8	9	10
11	12	13	14	15	16	17
18	19	20	21	22	23	24
25	26	27	28	29	30	

October

S	M	T	W	T	F	S
						1
2	3	4	5	6	7	8
9	10	11	12	13	14	15
16	17	18	19	20	21	22
23	24	25	26	27	28	29
30	31					

November

S	M	T	W	T	F	S
		1	2	3	4	5
6	7	8	9	10	11	12
13	14	15	16	17	18	19
20	21	22	23	24	25	26
27	28	29	30			

December

S	M	T	W	T	F	S
				1	2	3
4	5	6	7	8	9	10
11	12	13	14	15	16	17
18	19	20	21	22	23	24
25	26	27	28	29	30	31

January

S	M	T	W	T	F	S
1	2	3	4	5	6	7
8	9	10	11	12	13	14
15	16	17	18	19	20	21
22	23	24	25	26	27	28
29	30	31				

February

S	M	T	W	T	F	S
			1	2	3	4
5	6	7	8	9	10	11
12	13	14	15	16	17	18
19	20	21	22	23	24	25
26	27	28				

March

S	M	T	W	T	F	S
			1	2	3	4
5	6	7	8	9	10	11
12	13	14	15	16	17	18
19	20	21	22	23	24	25
26	27	28	29	30	31	

April

S	M	T	W	T	F	S
						1
2	3	4	5	6	7	8
9	10	11	12	13	14	15
16	17	18	19	20	21	22
23	24	25	26	27	28	29
30						

May

S	M	T	W	T	F	S
	1	2	3	4	5	6
7	8	9	10	11	12	13
14	15	16	17	18	19	20
21	22	23	24	25	26	27
28	29	30	31			

June

S	M	T	W	T	F	S
				1	2	3
4	5	6	7	8	9	10
11	12	13	14	15	16	17
18	19	20	21	22	23	24
25	26	27	28	29	30	

US FEDERAL HOLIDAYS

MONDAY	4 JUL	INDEPENDENCE DAY
MONDAY	5 SEP	LABOR DAY
FRIDAY	11 NOV	VETERANS DAY
THURSDAY	24 NOV	THANKSGIVING DAY
MONDAY	26 DEC	CHRISTMAS DAY
MONDAY	2 JAN	NEW YEAR'S DAY
MONDAY	16 JAN	MARTIN LUTHER KING JR. DAY
MONDAY	29 MAY	MEMORIAL DAY

UK FEDERAL HOLIDAYS

MONDAY	29 AUG	SUMMER BANK HOLIDAY
MONDAY	26 DEC	BOXING DAY
TUESDAY	27 DEC	CHRISTMAS DAY
MONDAY	2 JAN	NEW YEAR'S DAY
FRIDAY	7 APR	GOOD FRIDAY
MONDAY	10 APR	EASTER MONDAY
MONDAY	1 MAY	EARLY MAY BANK HOLIDAY
MONDAY	29 MAY	SPRING BANK HOLIDAY

July 2022

Sunday	Monday	Tuesday	Wednesday
3	4	5	6
10	11	12	13
17	18	19	20
24 / 31	25	26	27

"The pessimist sees difficulty in every opportunity. The optimist sees the opportunity in every difficulty." -Winston Churchill

Thursday	Friday	Saturday
	1	2
7	8	9
14	15	16
21	22	23
28	29	30

Notes

27 Mon. Jun 27, 2022

○
○
○
○
○
○
○
○
○
○

28 Tue. Jun 28, 2022

○
○
○
○
○
○
○
○
○
○

29 Wed. Jun 29, 2022

○
○
○
○
○
○
○
○
○
○

30 Thu. Jun 30, 2022

○
○
○
○
○
○
○
○
○
○

01 Fri. Jul 1, 2022

○
○
○
○
○
○
○
○
○
○

02 Sat. Jul 2, 2022

03 Sun. Jul 3, 2022

04 Mon. Jul 4, 2022

○
○
○
○
○
○
○
○
○
○

05 Tue. Jul 5, 2022

○
○
○
○
○
○
○
○
○
○

06 Wed. Jul 6, 2022

○
○
○
○
○
○
○
○
○
○

07 Thu. Jul 7, 2022

○
○
○
○
○
○
○
○
○
○

08 Fri. Jul 8, 2022

○
○
○
○
○
○
○
○
○
○

09 Sat. Jul 9, 2022

10 Sun. Jul 10, 2022

11 Mon. Jul 11, 2022

○
○
○
○
○
○
○
○
○
○

12 Tue. Jul 12, 2022

○
○
○
○
○
○
○
○
○
○

13 Wed. Jul 13, 2022

○
○
○
○
○
○
○
○
○
○

14 Thu. Jul 14, 2022

○
○
○
○
○
○
○
○
○
○

15 Fri. Jul 15, 2022

○
○
○
○
○
○
○
○
○
○

16 Sat. Jul 16, 2022

17 Sun. Jul 17, 2022

18 Mon. Jul 18, 2022

○
○
○
○
○
○
○
○
○
○

19 Tue. Jul 19, 2022

○
○
○
○
○
○
○
○
○
○

20 Wed. Jul 20, 2022

○
○
○
○
○
○
○
○
○
○

21 Thu. Jul 21, 2022

○
○
○
○
○
○
○
○
○
○

22 Fri. Jul 22, 2022

○
○
○
○
○
○
○
○
○
○

23 Sat. Jul 23, 2022

24 Sun. Jul 24, 2022

25 Mon. Jul 25, 2022

○
○
○
○
○
○
○
○
○
○

26 Tue. Jul 26, 2022

○
○
○
○
○
○
○
○
○
○

27 Wed. Jul 27, 2022

○
○
○
○
○
○
○
○
○
○

28 Thu. Jul 28, 2022

○
○
○
○
○
○
○
○
○
○

29 Fri. Jul 29, 2022

○
○
○
○
○
○
○
○
○
○

30 Sat. Jul 30, 2022

31 Sun. Jul 31, 2022

August 2022

Sunday	Monday	Tuesday	Wednesday
	1	2	3
7	8	9	10
14	15	16	17
21	22	23	24
28	29	30	31

"It's not whether you get knocked down, it's whether you get up."
-Vince Lombardi

Thursday 4	Friday 5	Saturday 6	Notes
11	12	13	
18	19	20	
25	26	27	

01 Mon. Aug 1, 2022

○
○
○
○
○
○
○
○
○
○

02 Tue. Aug 2, 2022

○
○
○
○
○
○
○
○
○
○

03 Wed. Aug 3, 2022

○
○
○
○
○
○
○
○
○
○

04 Thu. Aug 4, 2022

○
○
○
○
○
○
○
○
○
○

05 Fri. Aug 5, 2022

○
○
○
○
○
○
○
○
○
○

06 Sat. Aug 6, 2022

07 Sun. Aug 7, 2022

08 Mon. Aug 8, 2022

○
○
○
○
○
○
○
○
○
○

09 Tue. Aug 9, 2022

○
○
○
○
○
○
○
○
○
○

10 Wed. Aug 10, 2022

○
○
○
○
○
○
○
○
○
○

11 Thu. Aug 11, 2022

○
○
○
○
○
○
○
○
○
○

12 Fri. Aug 12, 2022

○
○
○
○
○
○
○
○
○
○

13 Sat. Aug 13, 2022

14 Sun. Aug 14, 2022

15 Mon. Aug 15, 2022

○
○
○
○
○
○
○
○
○
○

16 Tue. Aug 16, 2022

○
○
○
○
○
○
○
○
○
○

17 Wed. Aug 17, 2022

○
○
○
○
○
○
○
○
○
○

18 Thu. Aug 18, 2022

○
○
○
○
○
○
○
○
○
○

19 Fri. Aug 19, 2022

○
○
○
○
○
○
○
○
○
○

20 Sat. Aug 20, 2022

21 Sun. Aug 21, 2022

22 Mon. Aug 22, 2022

○
○
○
○
○
○
○
○
○
○
○

23 Tue. Aug 23, 2022

○
○
○
○
○
○
○
○
○
○
○

24 Wed. Aug 24, 2022

○
○
○
○
○
○
○
○
○
○
○

25 Thu. Aug 25, 2022

○
○
○
○
○
○
○
○
○
○

26 Fri. Aug 26, 2022

○
○
○
○
○
○
○
○
○
○

27 Sat. Aug 27, 2022

28 Sun. Aug 28, 2022

29 Mon. Aug 29, 2022

○
○
○
○
○
○
○
○
○
○

30 Tue. Aug 30, 2022

○
○
○
○
○
○
○
○
○
○

31 Wed. Aug 31, 2022

○
○
○
○
○
○
○
○
○
○

For a better month view this page is left blank.

September 2022

Sunday	Monday	Tuesday	Wednesday
4	5	6	7
11	12	13	14
18	19	20	21
25	26	27	28

"We may encounter many defeats but we must not be defeated."
-Maya Angelou

Thursday 1	Friday 2	Saturday 3
8	9	10
15	16	17
22	23	24
29	30	

Notes

_____
_____
_____
_____
_____
_____
_____
_____
_____
_____
_____
_____
_____
_____
_____
_____
_____
_____
_____
_____
_____
_____
_____
_____
_____
_____
_____

For a better week view this page is left blank.

01 Thu. Sep 1, 2022

○
○
○
○
○
○
○
○
○
○

02 Fri. Sep 2, 2022

○
○
○
○
○
○
○
○
○
○

03 Sat. Sep 3, 2022

04 Sun. Sep 4, 2022

05 Mon. Sep 5, 2022

○
○
○
○
○
○
○
○
○
○

06 Tue. Sep 6, 2022

○
○
○
○
○
○
○
○
○
○

07 Wed. Sep 7, 2022

○
○
○
○
○
○
○
○
○
○

08 Thu. Sep 8, 2022

- ○
- ○
- ○
- ○
- ○
- ○
- ○
- ○
- ○
- ○

09 Fri. Sep 9, 2022

- ○
- ○
- ○
- ○
- ○
- ○
- ○
- ○
- ○
- ○

10 Sat. Sep 10, 2022

11 Sun. Sep 11, 2022

12 Mon. Sep 12, 2022

○
○
○
○
○
○
○
○
○
○

13 Tue. Sep 13, 2022

○
○
○
○
○
○
○
○
○
○

14 Wed. Sep 14, 2022

○
○
○
○
○
○
○
○
○
○

15 Thu. Sep 15, 2022

○
○
○
○
○
○
○
○
○
○

16 Fri. Sep 16, 2022

○
○
○
○
○
○
○
○
○
○

17 Sat. Sep 17, 2022

18 Sun. Sep 18, 2022

19 Mon. Sep 19, 2022

- ○
- ○
- ○
- ○
- ○
- ○
- ○
- ○
- ○
- ○

20 Tue. Sep 20, 2022

- ○
- ○
- ○
- ○
- ○
- ○
- ○
- ○
- ○
- ○

21 Wed. Sep 21, 2022

- ○
- ○
- ○
- ○
- ○
- ○
- ○
- ○
- ○
- ○

22 Thu. Sep 22, 2022

○
○
○
○
○
○
○
○
○
○

23 Fri. Sep 23, 2022

○
○
○
○
○
○
○
○
○
○

24 Sat. Sep 24, 2022

25 Sun. Sep 25, 2022

26 Mon. Sep 26, 2022

○
○
○
○
○
○
○
○
○
○
○

27 Tue. Sep 27, 2022

○
○
○
○
○
○
○
○
○
○
○

28 Wed. Sep 28, 2022

○
○
○
○
○
○
○
○
○
○

29 Thu. Sep 29, 2022

- ○
- ○
- ○
- ○
- ○
- ○
- ○
- ○
- ○
- ○

30 Fri. Sep 30, 2022

- ○
- ○
- ○
- ○
- ○
- ○
- ○
- ○
- ○
- ○

01 Sat. Oct 1, 2022

02 Sun. Oct 2, 2022

October

2022

Sunday	Monday	Tuesday	Wednesday
2	3	4	5
9	10	11	12
16	17	18	19
23 30	24 31	25	26

"The only limit to our realization of tomorrow will be our doubts of today." -Franklin D. Roosevelt

Thursday	Friday	Saturday
		1
6	7	8
13	14	15
20	21	22
27	28	29

Notes

_____
_____
_____
_____
_____
_____
_____
_____
_____
_____
_____
_____
_____
_____
_____
_____
_____
_____
_____
_____
_____
_____
_____

03 Mon. Oct 3, 2022

○
○
○
○
○
○
○
○
○
○

04 Tue. Oct 4, 2022

○
○
○
○
○
○
○
○
○
○

05 Wed. Oct 5, 2022

○
○
○
○
○
○
○
○
○
○

06 Thu. Oct 6, 2022

○
○
○
○
○
○
○
○
○
○

07 Fri. Oct 7, 2022

○
○
○
○
○
○
○
○
○
○

08 Sat. Oct 8, 2022

09 Sun. Oct 9, 2022

10 Mon. Oct 10, 2022

○
○
○
○
○
○
○
○
○
○

11 Tue. Oct 11, 2022

○
○
○
○
○
○
○
○
○
○

12 Wed. Oct 12, 2022

○
○
○
○
○
○
○
○
○
○

13 Thu. Oct 13, 2022

○
○
○
○
○
○
○
○
○
○

14 Fri. Oct 14, 2022

○
○
○
○
○
○
○
○
○
○

15 Sat. Oct 15, 2022

16 Sun. Oct 16, 2022

17 Mon. Oct 17, 2022

○
○
○
○
○
○
○
○
○
○

18 Tue. Oct 18, 2022

○
○
○
○
○
○
○
○
○
○

19 Wed. Oct 19, 2022

○
○
○
○
○
○
○
○
○
○

20 Thu. Oct 20, 2022

○
○
○
○
○
○
○
○
○
○

21 Fri. Oct 21, 2022

○
○
○
○
○
○
○
○
○
○

22 Sat. Oct 22, 2022

23 Sun. Oct 23, 2022

24 Mon. Oct 24, 2022

○
○
○
○
○
○
○
○
○
○
○

25 Tue. Oct 25, 2022

○
○
○
○
○
○
○
○
○
○

26 Wed. Oct 26, 2022

○
○
○
○
○
○
○
○
○
○

27 Thu. Oct 27, 2022

○
○
○
○
○
○
○
○
○
○

28 Fri. Oct 28, 2022

○
○
○
○
○
○
○
○
○
○

29 Sat. Oct 29, 2022

30 Sun. Oct 30, 2022

November 2022

Sunday	Monday	Tuesday	Wednesday
		1	2
6	7	8	9
13	14	15	16
20	21	22	23
27	28	29	30

> *"The world breaks everyone, and afterward, some are strong at the broken places."* - Ernest Hemingway

Thursday 3	Friday 4	Saturday 5	Notes
10	11	12	
17	18	19	
24	25	26	

31 Mon. Oct 31, 2022 ⎯⎯⎯⎯⎯⎯⎯

⎯⎯⎯⎯⎯⎯⎯⎯⎯⎯ ○ ⎯⎯⎯⎯⎯⎯⎯
⎯⎯⎯⎯⎯⎯⎯⎯⎯⎯ ○ ⎯⎯⎯⎯⎯⎯⎯
⎯⎯⎯⎯⎯⎯⎯⎯⎯⎯ ○ ⎯⎯⎯⎯⎯⎯⎯
⎯⎯⎯⎯⎯⎯⎯⎯⎯⎯ ○ ⎯⎯⎯⎯⎯⎯⎯
⎯⎯⎯⎯⎯⎯⎯⎯⎯⎯ ○ ⎯⎯⎯⎯⎯⎯⎯
⎯⎯⎯⎯⎯⎯⎯⎯⎯⎯ ○ ⎯⎯⎯⎯⎯⎯⎯
⎯⎯⎯⎯⎯⎯⎯⎯⎯⎯ ○ ⎯⎯⎯⎯⎯⎯⎯
⎯⎯⎯⎯⎯⎯⎯⎯⎯⎯ ○ ⎯⎯⎯⎯⎯⎯⎯
⎯⎯⎯⎯⎯⎯⎯⎯⎯⎯ ○ ⎯⎯⎯⎯⎯⎯⎯
⎯⎯⎯⎯⎯⎯⎯⎯⎯⎯ ○ ⎯⎯⎯⎯⎯⎯⎯

01 Tue. Nov 1, 2022 ⎯⎯⎯⎯⎯⎯⎯

⎯⎯⎯⎯⎯⎯⎯⎯⎯⎯ ○ ⎯⎯⎯⎯⎯⎯⎯
⎯⎯⎯⎯⎯⎯⎯⎯⎯⎯ ○ ⎯⎯⎯⎯⎯⎯⎯
⎯⎯⎯⎯⎯⎯⎯⎯⎯⎯ ○ ⎯⎯⎯⎯⎯⎯⎯
⎯⎯⎯⎯⎯⎯⎯⎯⎯⎯ ○ ⎯⎯⎯⎯⎯⎯⎯
⎯⎯⎯⎯⎯⎯⎯⎯⎯⎯ ○ ⎯⎯⎯⎯⎯⎯⎯
⎯⎯⎯⎯⎯⎯⎯⎯⎯⎯ ○ ⎯⎯⎯⎯⎯⎯⎯
⎯⎯⎯⎯⎯⎯⎯⎯⎯⎯ ○ ⎯⎯⎯⎯⎯⎯⎯
⎯⎯⎯⎯⎯⎯⎯⎯⎯⎯ ○ ⎯⎯⎯⎯⎯⎯⎯
⎯⎯⎯⎯⎯⎯⎯⎯⎯⎯ ○ ⎯⎯⎯⎯⎯⎯⎯
⎯⎯⎯⎯⎯⎯⎯⎯⎯⎯ ○ ⎯⎯⎯⎯⎯⎯⎯

02 Wed. Nov 2, 2022 ⎯⎯⎯⎯⎯⎯⎯

⎯⎯⎯⎯⎯⎯⎯⎯⎯⎯ ○ ⎯⎯⎯⎯⎯⎯⎯
⎯⎯⎯⎯⎯⎯⎯⎯⎯⎯ ○ ⎯⎯⎯⎯⎯⎯⎯
⎯⎯⎯⎯⎯⎯⎯⎯⎯⎯ ○ ⎯⎯⎯⎯⎯⎯⎯
⎯⎯⎯⎯⎯⎯⎯⎯⎯⎯ ○ ⎯⎯⎯⎯⎯⎯⎯
⎯⎯⎯⎯⎯⎯⎯⎯⎯⎯ ○ ⎯⎯⎯⎯⎯⎯⎯
⎯⎯⎯⎯⎯⎯⎯⎯⎯⎯ ○ ⎯⎯⎯⎯⎯⎯⎯
⎯⎯⎯⎯⎯⎯⎯⎯⎯⎯ ○ ⎯⎯⎯⎯⎯⎯⎯
⎯⎯⎯⎯⎯⎯⎯⎯⎯⎯ ○ ⎯⎯⎯⎯⎯⎯⎯
⎯⎯⎯⎯⎯⎯⎯⎯⎯⎯ ○ ⎯⎯⎯⎯⎯⎯⎯
⎯⎯⎯⎯⎯⎯⎯⎯⎯⎯ ○ ⎯⎯⎯⎯⎯⎯⎯

03 Thu. Nov 3, 2022

○
○
○
○
○
○
○
○
○
○

04 Fri. Nov 4, 2022

○
○
○
○
○
○
○
○
○
○

05 Sat. Nov 5, 2022

06 Sun. Nov 6, 2022

07   **Mon. Nov 7, 2022**

    ○
    ○
    ○
    ○
    ○
    ○
    ○
    ○
    ○
    ○

08   **Tue. Nov 8, 2022**

    ○
    ○
    ○
    ○
    ○
    ○
    ○
    ○
    ○
    ○

09   **Wed. Nov 9, 2022**

    ○
    ○
    ○
    ○
    ○
    ○
    ○
    ○
    ○
    ○

10 Thu. Nov 10, 2022

○
○
○
○
○
○
○
○
○
○

11 Fri. Nov 11, 2022

○
○
○
○
○
○
○
○
○
○

12 Sat. Nov 12, 2022

13 Sun. Nov 13, 2022

14   **Mon. Nov 14, 2022**

○
○
○
○
○
○
○
○
○
○

15   **Tue. Nov 15, 2022**

○
○
○
○
○
○
○
○
○
○

16   **Wed. Nov 16, 2022**

○
○
○
○
○
○
○
○
○
○

17 Thu. Nov 17, 2022

○
○
○
○
○
○
○
○
○
○

18 Fri. Nov 18, 2022

○
○
○
○
○
○
○
○
○
○

19 Sat. Nov 19, 2022

20 Sun. Nov 20, 2022

21 Mon. Nov 21, 2022

○
○
○
○
○
○
○
○
○
○

22 Tue. Nov 22, 2022

○
○
○
○
○
○
○
○
○
○

23 Wed. Nov 23, 2022

○
○
○
○
○
○
○
○
○
○

24 Thu. Nov 24, 2022

○
○
○
○
○
○
○
○
○
○

25 Fri. Nov 25, 2022

○
○
○
○
○
○
○
○
○
○

26 Sat. Nov 26, 2022

27 Sun. Nov 27, 2022

28   **Mon. Nov 28, 2022**

○
○
○
○
○
○
○
○
○
○
○

29   **Tue. Nov 29, 2022**

○
○
○
○
○
○
○
○
○
○
○

30   **Wed. Nov 30, 2022**

○
○
○
○
○
○
○
○
○
○
○

For a better month view this page is left blank.

December   2022

Sunday	Monday	Tuesday	Wednesday
4	5	6	7
11	12	13	14
18	19	20	21
25	26	27	28

"A truly strong person does not need the approval of others any more than a lion needs the approval of sheep." -Vernon Howard

Thursday 1	Friday 2	Saturday 3
8	9	10
15	16	17
22	23	24
29	30	31

Notes

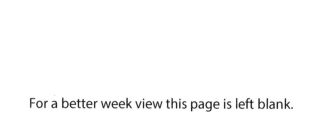
For a better week view this page is left blank.

01 Thu. Dec 1, 2022

○
○
○
○
○
○
○
○
○
○

02 Fri. Dec 2, 2022

○
○
○
○
○
○
○
○
○
○

03 Sat. Dec 3, 2022

04 Sun. Dec 4, 2022

05 Mon. Dec 5, 2022 ———————————————

———————————————
———————————————
———————————————
———————————————
———————————————
———————————————
———————————————
———————————————
———————————————
———————————————

○ ———————————
○ ———————————
○ ———————————
○ ———————————
○ ———————————
○ ———————————
○ ———————————
○ ———————————
○ ———————————
○ ———————————

06 Tue. Dec 6, 2022 ———————————————

———————————————
———————————————
———————————————
———————————————
———————————————
———————————————
———————————————
———————————————
———————————————
———————————————

○ ———————————
○ ———————————
○ ———————————
○ ———————————
○ ———————————
○ ———————————
○ ———————————
○ ———————————
○ ———————————
○ ———————————

07 Wed. Dec 7, 2022 ———————————————

———————————————
———————————————
———————————————
———————————————
———————————————
———————————————
———————————————
———————————————
———————————————
———————————————

○ ———————————
○ ———————————
○ ———————————
○ ———————————
○ ———————————
○ ———————————
○ ———————————
○ ———————————
○ ———————————
○ ———————————

08 Thu. Dec 8, 2022

○
○
○
○
○
○
○
○
○
○

09 Fri. Dec 9, 2022

○
○
○
○
○
○
○
○
○
○

10 Sat. Dec 10, 2022

11 Sun. Dec 11, 2022

12 Mon. Dec 12, 2022 ———————————————

———————————————————— ○ ————————————
———————————————————— ○ ————————————
———————————————————— ○ ————————————
———————————————————— ○ ————————————
———————————————————— ○ ————————————
———————————————————— ○ ————————————
———————————————————— ○ ————————————
———————————————————— ○ ————————————
———————————————————— ○ ————————————
———————————————————— ○ ————————————

13 Tue. Dec 13, 2022 ———————————————

———————————————————— ○ ————————————
———————————————————— ○ ————————————
———————————————————— ○ ————————————
———————————————————— ○ ————————————
———————————————————— ○ ————————————
———————————————————— ○ ————————————
———————————————————— ○ ————————————
———————————————————— ○ ————————————
———————————————————— ○ ————————————
———————————————————— ○ ————————————

14 Wed. Dec 14, 2022 ———————————————

———————————————————— ○ ————————————
———————————————————— ○ ————————————
———————————————————— ○ ————————————
———————————————————— ○ ————————————
———————————————————— ○ ————————————
———————————————————— ○ ————————————
———————————————————— ○ ————————————
———————————————————— ○ ————————————
———————————————————— ○ ————————————
———————————————————— ○ ————————————

15 Thu. Dec 15, 2022

○
○
○
○
○
○
○
○
○
○

16 Fri. Dec 16, 2022

○
○
○
○
○
○
○
○
○
○

17 Sat. Dec 17, 2022

18 Sun. Dec 18, 2022

19 Mon. Dec 19, 2022

○
○
○
○
○
○
○
○
○
○

20 Tue. Dec 20, 2022

○
○
○
○
○
○
○
○
○
○

21 Wed. Dec 21, 2022

○
○
○
○
○
○
○
○
○
○

22 Thu. Dec 22, 2022

○
○
○
○
○
○
○
○
○
○

23 Fri. Dec 23, 2022

○
○
○
○
○
○
○
○
○
○

24 Sat. Dec 24, 2022

25 Sun. Dec 25, 2022

26 Mon. Dec 26, 2022

○
○
○
○
○
○
○
○
○
○

27 Tue. Dec 27, 2022

○
○
○
○
○
○
○
○
○
○

28 Wed. Dec 28, 2022

○
○
○
○
○
○
○
○
○
○

29 Thu. Dec 29, 2022

○
○
○
○
○
○
○
○
○
○

30 Fri. Dec 30, 2022

○
○
○
○
○
○
○
○
○
○

31 Sat. Dec 31, 2022

01 Sun. Jan 1, 2023

January 2023

Sunday	Monday	Tuesday	Wednesday
1	2	3	4
8	9	10	11
15	16	17	18
22	23	24	25
29	30	31	

"Tough times never last, but tough people do." -Robert H. Schuller

Thursday	Friday	Saturday
5	6	7
12	13	14
19	20	21
26	27	28

Notes

_____
_____
_____
_____
_____
_____
_____
_____
_____
_____
_____
_____
_____
_____
_____
_____
_____
_____
_____
_____
_____
_____
_____
_____
_____

02 Mon. Jan 2, 2023

○
○
○
○
○
○
○
○
○
○
○

03 Tue. Jan 3, 2023

○
○
○
○
○
○
○
○
○
○

04 Wed. Jan 4, 2023

○
○
○
○
○
○
○
○
○
○

05 Thu. Jan 5, 2023

○
○
○
○
○
○
○
○
○
○

06 Fri. Jan 6, 2023

○
○
○
○
○
○
○
○
○
○

07 Sat. Jan 7, 2023

08 Sun. Jan 8, 2023

09 Mon. Jan 9, 2023

○
○
○
○
○
○
○
○
○
○

10 Tue. Jan 10, 2023

○
○
○
○
○
○
○
○
○
○

11 Wed. Jan 11, 2023

○
○
○
○
○
○
○
○
○
○

12 Thu. Jan 12, 2023

○
○
○
○
○
○
○
○
○
○

13 Fri. Jan 13, 2023

○
○
○
○
○
○
○
○
○
○

14 Sat. Jan 14, 2023

15 Sun. Jan 15, 2023

16 Mon. Jan 16, 2023

17 Tue. Jan 17, 2023

18 Wed. Jan 18, 2023

19 Thu. Jan 19, 2023

○
○
○
○
○
○
○
○
○
○

20 Fri. Jan 20, 2023

○
○
○
○
○
○
○
○
○
○

21 Sat. Jan 21, 2023

22 Sun. Jan 22, 2023

23 Mon. Jan 23, 2023 _____

_____ ○ _____
_____ ○ _____
_____ ○ _____
_____ ○ _____
_____ ○ _____
_____ ○ _____
_____ ○ _____
_____ ○ _____
_____ ○ _____
_____ ○ _____

24 Tue. Jan 24, 2023 _____

_____ ○ _____
_____ ○ _____
_____ ○ _____
_____ ○ _____
_____ ○ _____
_____ ○ _____
_____ ○ _____
_____ ○ _____
_____ ○ _____
_____ ○ _____

25 Wed. Jan 25, 2023 _____

_____ ○ _____
_____ ○ _____
_____ ○ _____
_____ ○ _____
_____ ○ _____
_____ ○ _____
_____ ○ _____
_____ ○ _____
_____ ○ _____
_____ ○ _____

26 Thu. Jan 26, 2023

○
○
○
○
○
○
○
○
○
○

27 Fri. Jan 27, 2023

○
○
○
○
○
○
○
○
○
○

28 Sat. Jan 28, 2023

29 Sun. Jan 29, 2023

30 Mon. Jan 30, 2023

31 Tue. Jan 31, 2023

01 Wed. Feb 1, 2023

For a better month view this page is left blank.

February   2023

Sunday	Monday	Tuesday	Wednesday
			1
5	6	7	8
12	13	14	15
19	20	21	22
26	27	28	

"Winning doesn't always mean being first. Winning means you're doing better than you've ever done before." –Bonnie Blair

Thursday 2	Friday 3	Saturday 4
9	10	11
16	17	18
23	24	25

Notes

For a better week view this page is left blank.

02 Thu. Feb 2, 2023

○
○
○
○
○
○
○
○
○
○

03 Fri. Feb 3, 2023

○
○
○
○
○
○
○
○
○
○

04 Sat. Feb 4, 2023

05 Sun. Feb 5, 2023

06 Mon. Feb 6, 2023

○
○
○
○
○
○
○
○
○
○

07 Tue. Feb 7, 2023

○
○
○
○
○
○
○
○
○
○

08 Wed. Feb 8, 2023

○
○
○
○
○
○
○
○
○
○

09 Thu. Feb 9, 2023

○
○
○
○
○
○
○
○
○
○

10 Fri. Feb 10, 2023

○
○
○
○
○
○
○
○
○
○

11 Sat. Feb 11, 2023

12 Sun. Feb 12, 2023

13 Mon. Feb 13, 2023

○
○
○
○
○
○
○
○
○
○

14 Tue. Feb 14, 2023

○
○
○
○
○
○
○
○
○
○

15 Wed. Feb 15, 2023

○
○
○
○
○
○
○
○
○
○

16 Thu. Feb 16, 2023

○
○
○
○
○
○
○
○
○
○

17 Fri. Feb 17, 2023

○
○
○
○
○
○
○
○
○
○

18 Sat. Feb 18, 2023

19 Sun. Feb 19, 2023

20 Mon. Feb 20, 2023

○
○
○
○
○
○
○
○
○
○

21 Tue. Feb 21, 2023

○
○
○
○
○
○
○
○
○
○

22 Wed. Feb 22, 2023

○
○
○
○
○
○
○
○
○
○

23 Thu. Feb 23, 2023

24 Fri. Feb 24, 2023

25 Sat. Feb 25, 2023

26 Sun. Feb 26, 2023

27 Mon. Feb 27, 2023 ———————————————

◯ ———————————
◯ ———————————
◯ ———————————
◯ ———————————
◯ ———————————
◯ ———————————
◯ ———————————
◯ ———————————
◯ ———————————
◯ ———————————

28 Tue. Feb 28, 2023 ———————————————

◯ ———————————
◯ ———————————
◯ ———————————
◯ ———————————
◯ ———————————
◯ ———————————
◯ ———————————
◯ ———————————
◯ ———————————
◯ ———————————

01 Wed. Mar 1, 2023 ———————————————

◯ ———————————
◯ ———————————
◯ ———————————
◯ ———————————
◯ ———————————
◯ ———————————
◯ ———————————
◯ ———————————
◯ ———————————
◯ ———————————

For a better month view this page is left blank.

March 2023

Sunday	Monday	Tuesday	Wednesday
			1
5	6	7	8
12	13	14	15
19	20	21	22
26	27	28	29

"There are always new, grander challenges to confront, and a true winner will embrace each one." -Mia Hamm

Thursday 2	Friday 3	Saturday 4
9	10	11
16	17	18
23	24	25
30	31	

Notes

_____
_____
_____
_____
_____
_____
_____
_____
_____
_____
_____
_____
_____
_____
_____
_____
_____
_____
_____
_____
_____
_____
_____

For a better week view this page is left blank.

02 Thu. Mar 2, 2023

○
○
○
○
○
○
○
○
○
○

03 Fri. Mar 3, 2023

○
○
○
○
○
○
○
○
○
○

04 Sat. Mar 4, 2023

05 Sun. Mar 5, 2023

06 Mon. Mar 6, 2023

○
○
○
○
○
○
○
○
○
○
○

07 Tue. Mar 7, 2023

○
○
○
○
○
○
○
○
○
○
○

08 Wed. Mar 8, 2023

○
○
○
○
○
○
○
○
○
○
○

09 Thu. Mar 9, 2023

○
○
○
○
○
○
○
○
○
○

10 Fri. Mar 10, 2023

○
○
○
○
○
○
○
○
○
○

11 Sat. Mar 11, 2023

12 Sun. Mar 12, 2023

13 Mon. Mar 13, 2023 —————————

○ —————————
○ —————————
○ —————————
○ —————————
○ —————————
○ —————————
○ —————————
○ —————————
○ —————————
○ —————————

14 Tue. Mar 14, 2023 —————————

○ —————————
○ —————————
○ —————————
○ —————————
○ —————————
○ —————————
○ —————————
○ —————————
○ —————————
○ —————————

15 Wed. Mar 15, 2023 —————————

○ —————————
○ —————————
○ —————————
○ —————————
○ —————————
○ —————————
○ —————————
○ —————————
○ —————————
○ —————————

16 Thu. Mar 16, 2023

○
○
○
○
○
○
○
○
○
○

17 Fri. Mar 17, 2023

○
○
○
○
○
○
○
○
○
○

18 Sat. Mar 18, 2023

19 Sun. Mar 19, 2023

20 Mon. Mar 20, 2023

○
○
○
○
○
○
○
○
○
○

21 Tue. Mar 21, 2023

○
○
○
○
○
○
○
○
○
○

22 Wed. Mar 22, 2023

○
○
○
○
○
○
○
○
○
○

23 Thu. Mar 23, 2023

○
○
○
○
○
○
○
○
○
○

24 Fri. Mar 24, 2023

○
○
○
○
○
○
○
○
○
○

25 Sat. Mar 25, 2023

26 Sun. Mar 26, 2023

27 Mon. Mar 27, 2023 —————————————

————————————————— ○ —————————————
————————————————— ○ —————————————
————————————————— ○ —————————————
————————————————— ○ —————————————
————————————————— ○ —————————————
————————————————— ○ —————————————
————————————————— ○ —————————————
————————————————— ○ —————————————
————————————————— ○ —————————————
————————————————— ○ —————————————

28 Tue. Mar 28, 2023 —————————————

————————————————— ○ —————————————
————————————————— ○ —————————————
————————————————— ○ —————————————
————————————————— ○ —————————————
————————————————— ○ —————————————
————————————————— ○ —————————————
————————————————— ○ —————————————
————————————————— ○ —————————————
————————————————— ○ —————————————
————————————————— ○ —————————————

29 Wed. Mar 29, 2023 —————————————

————————————————— ○ —————————————
————————————————— ○ —————————————
————————————————— ○ —————————————
————————————————— ○ —————————————
————————————————— ○ —————————————
————————————————— ○ —————————————
————————————————— ○ —————————————
————————————————— ○ —————————————
————————————————— ○ —————————————
————————————————— ○ —————————————

30 Thu. Mar 30, 2023

○
○
○
○
○
○
○
○
○
○

31 Fri. Mar 31, 2023

○
○
○
○
○
○
○
○
○
○

01 Sat. Apr 1, 2023

02 Sun. Apr 2, 2023

April 2023

Sunday	Monday	Tuesday	Wednesday
2	3	4	5
9	10	11	12
16	17	18	19
23 / 30	24	25	26

"Winning isn't everything, but wanting it is." -Arnold Palmer

Thursday	Friday	Saturday
		1
6	7	8
13	14	15
20	21	22
27	28	29

Notes

_____
_____
_____
_____
_____
_____
_____
_____
_____
_____
_____
_____
_____
_____
_____
_____
_____
_____
_____
_____
_____
_____
_____
_____
_____

03 | Mon. Apr 3, 2023

○
○
○
○
○
○
○
○
○
○

04 | Tue. Apr 4, 2023

○
○
○
○
○
○
○
○
○
○

05 | Wed. Apr 5, 2023

○
○
○
○
○
○
○
○
○
○

06 Thu. Apr 6, 2023

○
○
○
○
○
○
○
○
○
○

07 Fri. Apr 7, 2023

○
○
○
○
○
○
○
○
○
○

08 Sat. Apr 8, 2023

09 Sun. Apr 9, 2023

10 Mon. Apr 10, 2023

○
○
○
○
○
○
○
○
○
○

11 Tue. Apr 11, 2023

○
○
○
○
○
○
○
○
○
○

12 Wed. Apr 12, 2023

○
○
○
○
○
○
○
○
○
○

13 Thu. Apr 13, 2023 _____

_____ ○ _____
_____ ○ _____
_____ ○ _____
_____ ○ _____
_____ ○ _____
_____ ○ _____
_____ ○ _____
_____ ○ _____
_____ ○ _____
_____ ○ _____

14 Fri. Apr 14, 2023 _____

_____ ○ _____
_____ ○ _____
_____ ○ _____
_____ ○ _____
_____ ○ _____
_____ ○ _____
_____ ○ _____
_____ ○ _____
_____ ○ _____
_____ ○ _____

15 Sat. Apr 15, 2023   **16** Sun. Apr 16, 2023

17 Mon. Apr 17, 2023

○
○
○
○
○
○
○
○
○
○

18 Tue. Apr 18, 2023

○
○
○
○
○
○
○
○
○
○

19 Wed. Apr 19, 2023

○
○
○
○
○
○
○
○
○
○

20 Thu. Apr 20, 2023

○
○
○
○
○
○
○
○
○
○

21 Fri. Apr 21, 2023

○
○
○
○
○
○
○
○
○
○

22 Sat. Apr 22, 2023

23 Sun. Apr 23, 2023

24 Mon. Apr 24, 2023

25 Tue. Apr 25, 2023

26 Wed. Apr 26, 2023

27 Thu. Apr 27, 2023

28 Fri. Apr 28, 2023

29 Sat. Apr 29, 2023

30 Sun. Apr 30, 2023

May

2023

Sunday	Monday	Tuesday	Wednesday
	1	2	3
7	8	9	10
14	15	16	17
21	22	23	24
28	29	30	31

"The bamboo that bends is stronger than the oak that resists." -Japanese Proverb

Thursday 4	Friday 5	Saturday 6
11	12	13
18	19	20
25	26	27

Notes

_____
_____
_____
_____
_____
_____
_____
_____
_____
_____
_____
_____
_____
_____
_____
_____
_____
_____
_____
_____
_____
_____
_____

01 Mon. May 1, 2023 ⎯⎯⎯⎯⎯⎯⎯⎯⎯⎯

⎯⎯⎯⎯⎯⎯⎯⎯⎯⎯ ○ ⎯⎯⎯⎯⎯⎯⎯⎯⎯⎯
⎯⎯⎯⎯⎯⎯⎯⎯⎯⎯ ○ ⎯⎯⎯⎯⎯⎯⎯⎯⎯⎯
⎯⎯⎯⎯⎯⎯⎯⎯⎯⎯ ○ ⎯⎯⎯⎯⎯⎯⎯⎯⎯⎯
⎯⎯⎯⎯⎯⎯⎯⎯⎯⎯ ○ ⎯⎯⎯⎯⎯⎯⎯⎯⎯⎯
⎯⎯⎯⎯⎯⎯⎯⎯⎯⎯ ○ ⎯⎯⎯⎯⎯⎯⎯⎯⎯⎯
⎯⎯⎯⎯⎯⎯⎯⎯⎯⎯ ○ ⎯⎯⎯⎯⎯⎯⎯⎯⎯⎯
⎯⎯⎯⎯⎯⎯⎯⎯⎯⎯ ○ ⎯⎯⎯⎯⎯⎯⎯⎯⎯⎯
⎯⎯⎯⎯⎯⎯⎯⎯⎯⎯ ○ ⎯⎯⎯⎯⎯⎯⎯⎯⎯⎯
⎯⎯⎯⎯⎯⎯⎯⎯⎯⎯ ○ ⎯⎯⎯⎯⎯⎯⎯⎯⎯⎯
⎯⎯⎯⎯⎯⎯⎯⎯⎯⎯ ○ ⎯⎯⎯⎯⎯⎯⎯⎯⎯⎯

02 Tue. May 2, 2023 ⎯⎯⎯⎯⎯⎯⎯⎯⎯⎯

⎯⎯⎯⎯⎯⎯⎯⎯⎯⎯ ○ ⎯⎯⎯⎯⎯⎯⎯⎯⎯⎯
⎯⎯⎯⎯⎯⎯⎯⎯⎯⎯ ○ ⎯⎯⎯⎯⎯⎯⎯⎯⎯⎯
⎯⎯⎯⎯⎯⎯⎯⎯⎯⎯ ○ ⎯⎯⎯⎯⎯⎯⎯⎯⎯⎯
⎯⎯⎯⎯⎯⎯⎯⎯⎯⎯ ○ ⎯⎯⎯⎯⎯⎯⎯⎯⎯⎯
⎯⎯⎯⎯⎯⎯⎯⎯⎯⎯ ○ ⎯⎯⎯⎯⎯⎯⎯⎯⎯⎯
⎯⎯⎯⎯⎯⎯⎯⎯⎯⎯ ○ ⎯⎯⎯⎯⎯⎯⎯⎯⎯⎯
⎯⎯⎯⎯⎯⎯⎯⎯⎯⎯ ○ ⎯⎯⎯⎯⎯⎯⎯⎯⎯⎯
⎯⎯⎯⎯⎯⎯⎯⎯⎯⎯ ○ ⎯⎯⎯⎯⎯⎯⎯⎯⎯⎯
⎯⎯⎯⎯⎯⎯⎯⎯⎯⎯ ○ ⎯⎯⎯⎯⎯⎯⎯⎯⎯⎯
⎯⎯⎯⎯⎯⎯⎯⎯⎯⎯ ○ ⎯⎯⎯⎯⎯⎯⎯⎯⎯⎯

03 Wed. May 3, 2023 ⎯⎯⎯⎯⎯⎯⎯⎯⎯⎯

⎯⎯⎯⎯⎯⎯⎯⎯⎯⎯ ○ ⎯⎯⎯⎯⎯⎯⎯⎯⎯⎯
⎯⎯⎯⎯⎯⎯⎯⎯⎯⎯ ○ ⎯⎯⎯⎯⎯⎯⎯⎯⎯⎯
⎯⎯⎯⎯⎯⎯⎯⎯⎯⎯ ○ ⎯⎯⎯⎯⎯⎯⎯⎯⎯⎯
⎯⎯⎯⎯⎯⎯⎯⎯⎯⎯ ○ ⎯⎯⎯⎯⎯⎯⎯⎯⎯⎯
⎯⎯⎯⎯⎯⎯⎯⎯⎯⎯ ○ ⎯⎯⎯⎯⎯⎯⎯⎯⎯⎯
⎯⎯⎯⎯⎯⎯⎯⎯⎯⎯ ○ ⎯⎯⎯⎯⎯⎯⎯⎯⎯⎯
⎯⎯⎯⎯⎯⎯⎯⎯⎯⎯ ○ ⎯⎯⎯⎯⎯⎯⎯⎯⎯⎯
⎯⎯⎯⎯⎯⎯⎯⎯⎯⎯ ○ ⎯⎯⎯⎯⎯⎯⎯⎯⎯⎯
⎯⎯⎯⎯⎯⎯⎯⎯⎯⎯ ○ ⎯⎯⎯⎯⎯⎯⎯⎯⎯⎯
⎯⎯⎯⎯⎯⎯⎯⎯⎯⎯ ○ ⎯⎯⎯⎯⎯⎯⎯⎯⎯⎯

04 Thu. May 4, 2023

○
○
○
○
○
○
○
○
○
○

05 Fri. May 5, 2023

○
○
○
○
○
○
○
○
○
○

06 Sat. May 6, 2023

07 Sun. May 7, 2023

08 Mon. May 8, 2023

09 Tue. May 9, 2023

10 Wed. May 10, 2023

11 Thu. May 11, 2023

○
○
○
○
○
○
○
○
○
○

12 Fri. May 12, 2023

○
○
○
○
○
○
○
○
○
○

13 Sat. May 13, 2023

14 Sun. May 14, 2023

15 Mon. May 15, 2023 ⎯⎯⎯⎯⎯⎯⎯⎯

○
○
○
○
○
○
○
○
○
○

16 Tue. May 16, 2023 ⎯⎯⎯⎯⎯⎯⎯⎯

○
○
○
○
○
○
○
○
○
○

17 Wed. May 17, 2023 ⎯⎯⎯⎯⎯⎯⎯⎯

○
○
○
○
○
○
○
○
○
○

18 Thu. May 18, 2023

○
○
○
○
○
○
○
○
○
○

19 Fri. May 19, 2023

○
○
○
○
○
○
○
○
○
○

20 Sat. May 20, 2023

21 Sun. May 21, 2023

22 Mon. May 22, 2023

○
○
○
○
○
○
○
○
○
○

23 Tue. May 23, 2023

○
○
○
○
○
○
○
○
○
○

24 Wed. May 24, 2023

○
○
○
○
○
○
○
○
○
○

25 Thu. May 25, 2023

26 Fri. May 26, 2023

27 Sat. May 27, 2023

28 Sun. May 28, 2023

29 Mon. May 29, 2023

30 Tue. May 30, 2023

31 Wed. May 31, 2023

For a better month view this page is left blank.

June 2023

Sunday	Monday	Tuesday	Wednesday
4	5	6	7
11	12	13	14
18	19	20	21
25	26	27	28

"The bamboo that bends is stronger than the oak that resists." -Japanese Proverb

Thursday 1	Friday 2	Saturday 3
8	9	10
15	16	17
22	23	24
29	30	

Notes

_____
_____
_____
_____
_____
_____
_____
_____
_____
_____
_____
_____
_____
_____
_____
_____
_____
_____
_____
_____
_____
_____
_____

For a better week view this page is left blank.

01 Thu. Jun 1, 2023

○
○
○
○
○
○
○
○
○
○

02 Fri. Jun 2, 2023

○
○
○
○
○
○
○
○
○
○

03 Sat. Jun 3, 2023

04 Sun. Jun 4, 2023

05 Mon. Jun 5, 2023

○
○
○
○
○
○
○
○
○
○

06 Tue. Jun 6, 2023

○
○
○
○
○
○
○
○
○
○

07 Wed. Jun 7, 2023

○
○
○
○
○
○
○
○
○
○

08 Thu. Jun 8, 2023

○
○
○
○
○
○
○
○
○
○

09 Fri. Jun 9, 2023

○
○
○
○
○
○
○
○
○
○

10 Sat. Jun 10, 2023

11 Sun. Jun 11, 2023

12 Mon. Jun 12, 2023

○
○
○
○
○
○
○
○
○
○

13 Tue. Jun 13, 2023

○
○
○
○
○
○
○
○
○
○

14 Wed. Jun 14, 2023

○
○
○
○
○
○
○
○
○
○

15 Thu. Jun 15, 2023

○
○
○
○
○
○
○
○
○
○

16 Fri. Jun 16, 2023

○
○
○
○
○
○
○
○
○
○

17 Sat. Jun 17, 2023

18 Sun. Jun 18, 2023

19 Mon. Jun 19, 2023

○
○
○
○
○
○
○
○
○
○

20 Tue. Jun 20, 2023

○
○
○
○
○
○
○
○
○
○

21 Wed. Jun 21, 2023

○
○
○
○
○
○
○
○
○
○

22 Thu. Jun 22, 2023

○
○
○
○
○
○
○
○
○
○

23 Fri. Jun 23, 2023

○
○
○
○
○
○
○
○
○
○

24 Sat. Jun 24, 2023

25 Sun. Jun 25, 2023

26 Mon. Jun 26, 2023

○
○
○
○
○
○
○
○
○
○

27 Tue. Jun 27, 2023

○
○
○
○
○
○
○
○
○
○

28 Wed. Jun 28, 2023

○
○
○
○
○
○
○
○
○
○

29 Thu. Jun 29, 2023

○
○
○
○
○
○
○
○
○
○

30 Fri. Jun 30, 2023

○
○
○
○
○
○
○
○
○
○

01 Sat. Jul 1, 2023

02 Sun. Jul 2, 2023

SCAN ME

Made in the USA
Monee, IL
20 May 2022

96797202R00083